# TEETH AND TUSKS

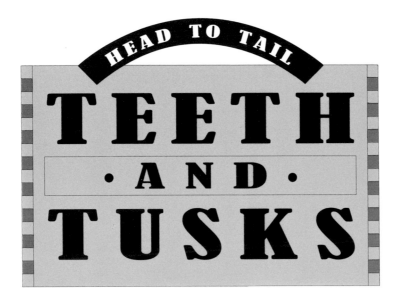

# HEAD TO TAIL

# TEETH · AND · TUSKS

WRITTEN BY
THERESA GREENAWAY

SCIENTIFIC CONSULTANT JOYCE POPE
ILLUSTRATED BY ANN SAVAGE,
JULIAN AND JANET BAKER

RSVP

RAINTREE
STECK-VAUGHN
PUBLISHERS
The Steck-Vaughn Company

Austin, Texas

**Library of Congress Cataloging-in-Publication Data**

Greenaway, Theresa, 1947–
Teeth and tusks / written by Theresa Greenaway;
illustrated by Ann Savage, Julian and Janet Baker.
p. cm. — (Head to tail)
Includes index.
ISBN 0-8114-8269-3
1. Teeth—Juvenile literature. 2. Tusks—Juvenile literature.
3. Antlers—Juvenile literature. 4. Animals—Juvenile literature.
[1. Teeth. 2. Tusks. 3. Antlers. 4. Animals]
I. Savage, Ann, 1951– ill. II. Baker, Julian, 1956– ill.
III. Baker, Janet, 1957– ill. IV. Title.
V. Series: Greenaway, Theresa, 1947- Head to Tail.
QL858.G74      1995
591.1'32—dc20
94–3496      CIP      AC

**Editors**: Wendy Madgwick and Kim Merlino
**Designer**: Janie Louise Hunt

Printed in Spain
1 2 3 4 5 6 7 8 9 0 LB 99 98 97 96 95 94

# Contents

# All About Teeth

You need teeth to chew your food before you eat it. So do animals. The shape of an animal's teeth tells you what it eats. Sharp front teeth bite off leaves and grass. Pointed teeth can stab and hold prey. Teeth with flat tops grind up tough food, like hay. Teeth are made of a hard bonelike material called dentine. They are covered with a hard, shiny material called enamel.

▼ **Wolf** Wolves eat meat. A wolf uses its sharp cheek teeth to cut off chunks of meat. It nibbles at tough parts with its front teeth.

## ▲ Chimpanzee

A chimpanzee's teeth
are a lot like your teeth. Chimpanzees
eat all kinds of food. They can chew
fruit, nuts, and meat with their teeth.

**▼ Giant Anteater** A giant
anteater has no teeth at all!
It eats hundreds of ants. The
anteater squashes the ants on
hard lumps on the roof of its
mouth.

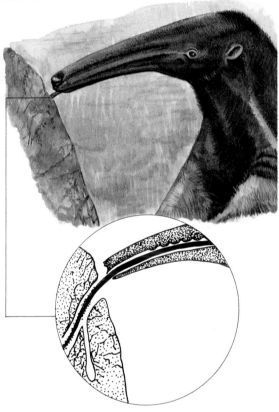

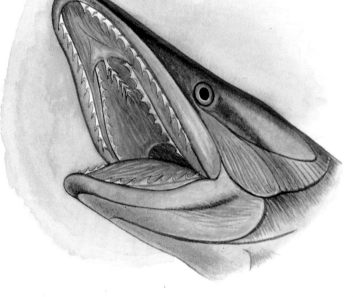

**▲ Pirarucu** A pirarucu is a large
fish. It lives in tropical rivers and
eats other fish. It has lots of
teeth! It has teeth in its jaws and
teeth on its tongue. It even has
teeth on the roof of its mouth.

**▼ Camel** The camel lives
in the desert. It eats prickly
desert plants. It chews them
with its large molars.

7

# All About Tusks

Tusks are teeth that have grown very big. They can be seen even when the animal shuts its mouth. Often only male animals have tusks. Tusks make them look fierce. Animals use their tusks in many ways. Some animals use them to dig up food. Others use them when they fight.

▼ **Deinotherium** This animal lived on Earth a long time ago. It looked like an elephant. Its big tusks curved down toward the ground. Perhaps it used them to dig up tasty roots.

▶ **Elephants** There are two kinds of elephants alive today. They live in Africa and India. Elephants have large tusks that grow from their top jaw. Some people kill elephants for their tusks. They sell them for ivory to make jewelry and ornaments. Many people are trying to stop this.

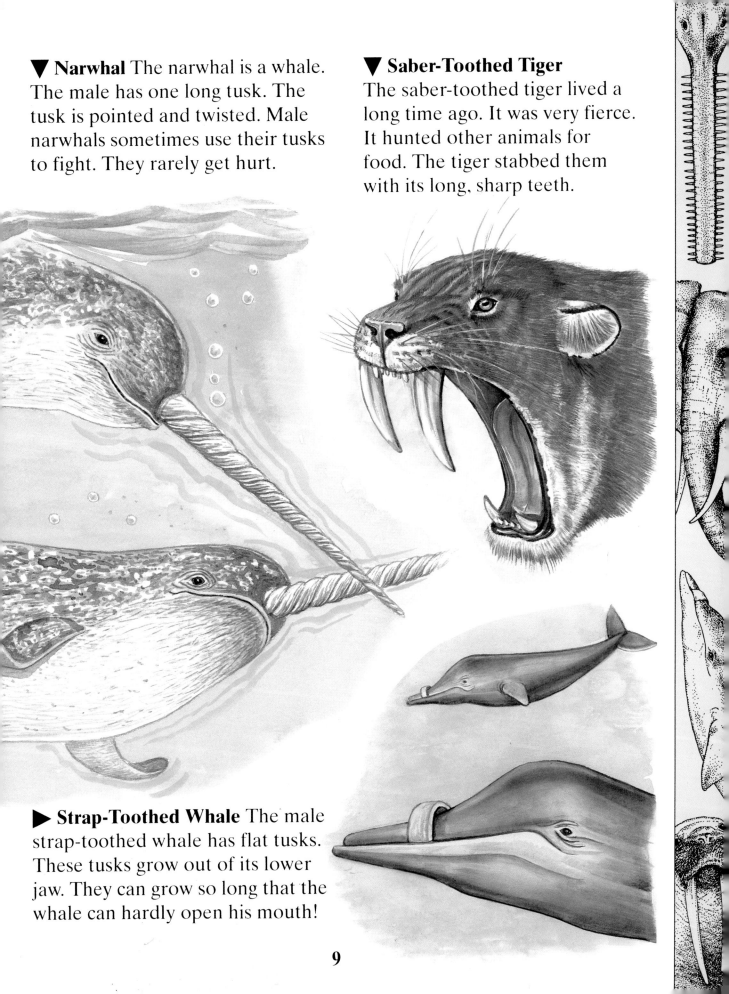

▼ **Narwhal** The narwhal is a whale. The male has one long tusk. The tusk is pointed and twisted. Male narwhals sometimes use their tusks to fight. They rarely get hurt.

▼ **Saber-Toothed Tiger** The saber-toothed tiger lived a long time ago. It was very fierce. It hunted other animals for food. The tiger stabbed them with its long, sharp teeth.

▶ **Strap-Toothed Whale** The male strap-toothed whale has flat tusks. These tusks grow out of its lower jaw. They can grow so long that the whale can hardly open his mouth!

# All About Antlers

**M**ale deer are called stags. They have antlers. Like teeth and tusks, antlers are made of a kind of bonelike material. Antlers grow on the top of a stag's head. Every year, a stag grows a new pair of antlers. They fall off at the end of winter. Each year the antlers get bigger. Stags often use their antlers to fight each other.

▲ **Moose** Moose have the largest antlers of any living deer. One male had a record pair that was 77 inches (2m) from tip to tip. The male with the largest antlers often wins stag fights.

▶ **Caribou** Caribou live in the Far North. It is very cold there in the winter. Snow covers the ground. Both female and male caribou have antlers. They use them to scrape away the snow to find plants to eat.

▼ **Irish Elk** This giant Irish elk stag lived a long time ago. It had the largest antlers of all times. They were about 13 feet (4m) across.

▼ **Pudu** The pudu has the smallest antlers — only a few inches long. Its antlers are straight.

▶ **Giraffe** Giraffes are not deer, but they have two bony horns, like antlers. Unlike antlers, they are not shed once a year. They are made of bone, covered with hair. Male giraffes' heads and horns grow thicker and bonier as they grow older. When male giraffes fight, they bash their heads together. Other animals, like rhinos, have horns, too. But they are not bony. They are made from hairlike material.

# In for the Kill

Some animals are predators, or hunters. Other animals are prey. A hunter has long pointed teeth on either side of its front teeth. These are called canines. The hunter often bites its prey in the neck or throat.

▶ **Tiger** The tiger is the biggest cat. It uses its large canine teeth to kill other animals. It has sharp-edged teeth at the sides of its mouth. These work like scissors. They cut up the meat into chunks.

▼ **Leopard Seal** A leopard seal swims in the ocean. It eats penguins. When it catches one, it takes the bird to the surface of the water. It holds the penguin in its teeth and shakes its head to kill the bird.

▲ **Weasel** The short-tailed weasel is small but very fierce. It often catches animals much larger than itself. A weasel bites the back of an animal's neck to kill it.

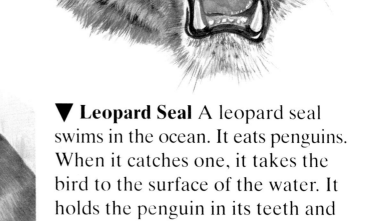

**▼ Ground Beetle** Even beetles can be fierce. This ground beetle hunts other small animals. It catches them in its toothy jaws.

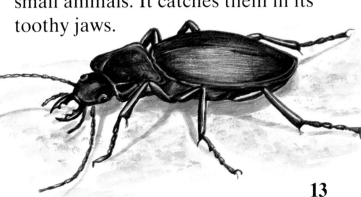

**▲ Crocodile** Crocodiles' teeth are shaped like cones. A crocodile lies in a river. It waits for an animal to come for a drink. It grabs the animal with its teeth. The crocodile then dives down beneath the water and drowns its prey.

# Meat Cleavers

Animals that eat meat also have sharp teeth at the sides of their mouths. Their sharp edges slide over each other like scissor blades. They slice food into small pieces. Some meat-eaters' jaws and teeth are very strong. They can even crunch up bones.

▶ **Tiger Shark** The tiger shark's teeth have tips like daggers and bases like saws. The shark can eat most animals. Even a turtle inside a hard shell is not safe.

◀ **Fossa** The fossa lives in the jungles of Madagascar, a large island near Africa. It is about the size of a mountain lion. The fossa feeds on birds and small animals.

14

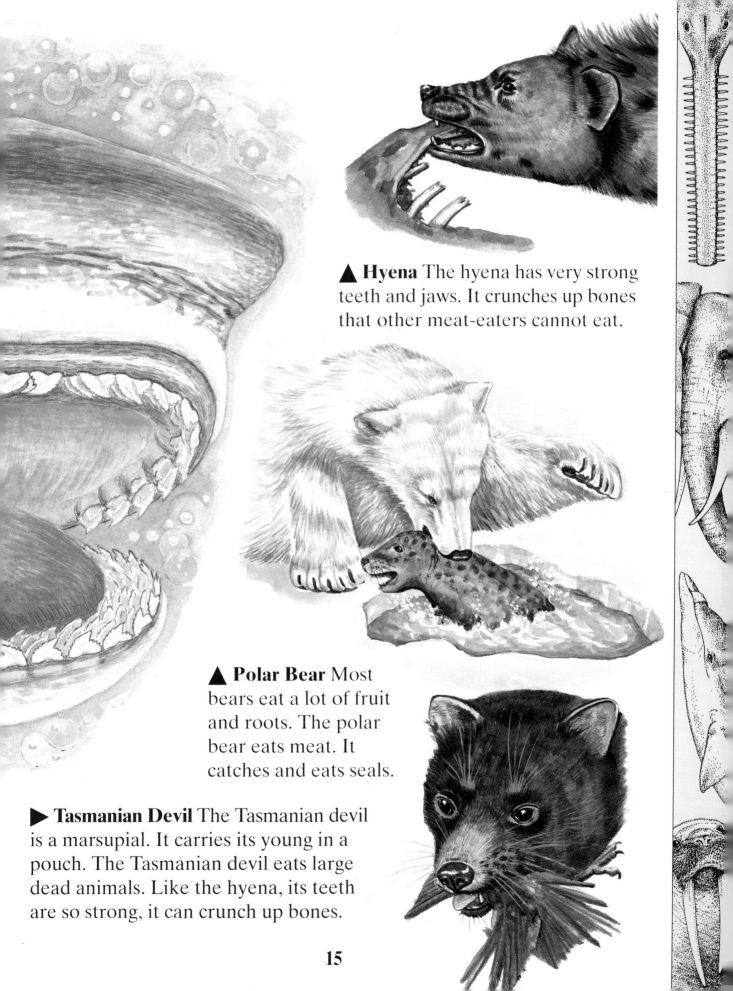

▲ **Hyena** The hyena has very strong teeth and jaws. It crunches up bones that other meat-eaters cannot eat.

▲ **Polar Bear** Most bears eat a lot of fruit and roots. The polar bear eats meat. It catches and eats seals.

▶ **Tasmanian Devil** The Tasmanian devil is a marsupial. It carries its young in a pouch. The Tasmanian devil eats large dead animals. Like the hyena, its teeth are so strong, it can crunch up bones.

# Fighting Fangs

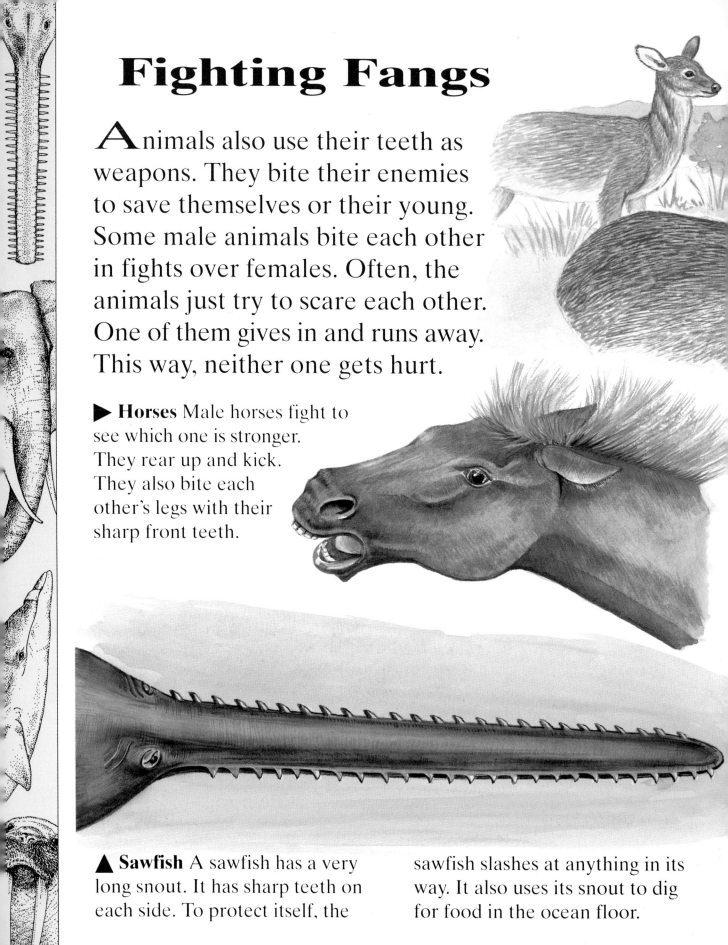

Animals also use their teeth as weapons. They bite their enemies to save themselves or their young. Some male animals bite each other in fights over females. Often, the animals just try to scare each other. One of them gives in and runs away. This way, neither one gets hurt.

▶ **Horses** Male horses fight to see which one is stronger. They rear up and kick. They also bite each other's legs with their sharp front teeth.

▲ **Sawfish** A sawfish has a very long snout. It has sharp teeth on each side. To protect itself, the sawfish slashes at anything in its way. It also uses its snout to dig for food in the ocean floor.

**▲ Musk Deer** The musk deer stag has two long, canine teeth like daggers. Sometimes males get hurt when they fight.

**▼ Peccary** The collared peccary lives in the Amazon rain forests. It has short, sharp tusks. Each peccary has its own home space called a territory. If another peccary comes into that space, the animals fight.

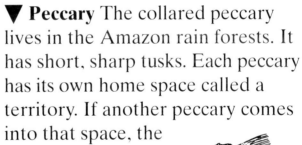

**◄ Beaked Whale** The beaked whale has a pair of tusks on its lower jaw. Male whales sometimes fight to win a female. A male's back often has old scars from earlier fights.

# Just the Job

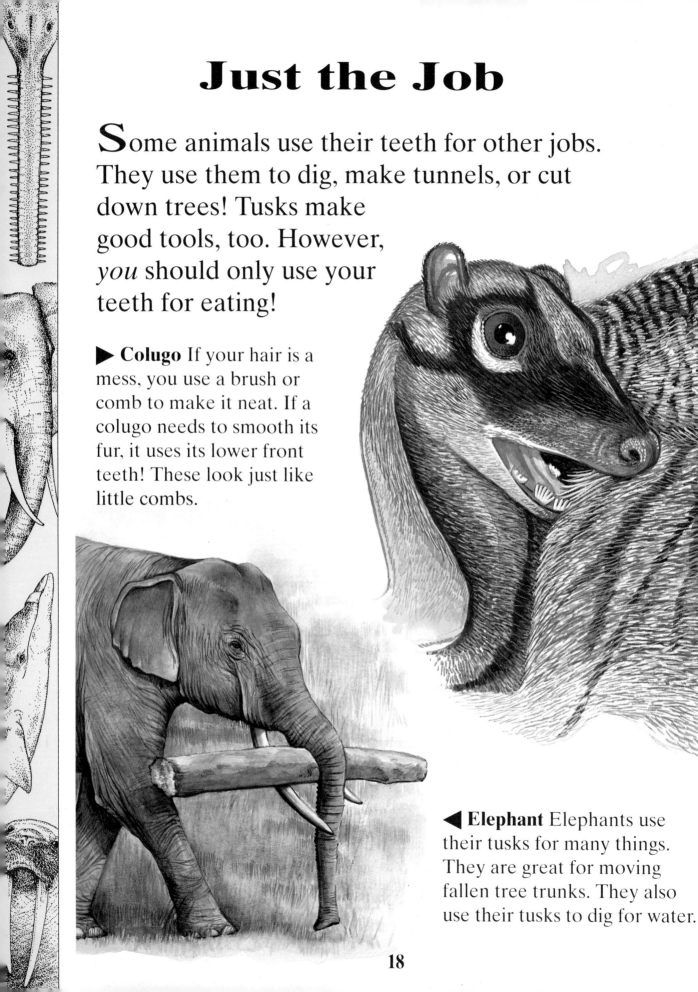

Some animals use their teeth for other jobs. They use them to dig, make tunnels, or cut down trees! Tusks make good tools, too. However, *you* should only use your teeth for eating!

▶ **Colugo** If your hair is a mess, you use a brush or comb to make it neat. If a colugo needs to smooth its fur, it uses its lower front teeth! These look just like little combs.

◀ **Elephant** Elephants use their tusks for many things. They are great for moving fallen tree trunks. They also use their tusks to dig for water.

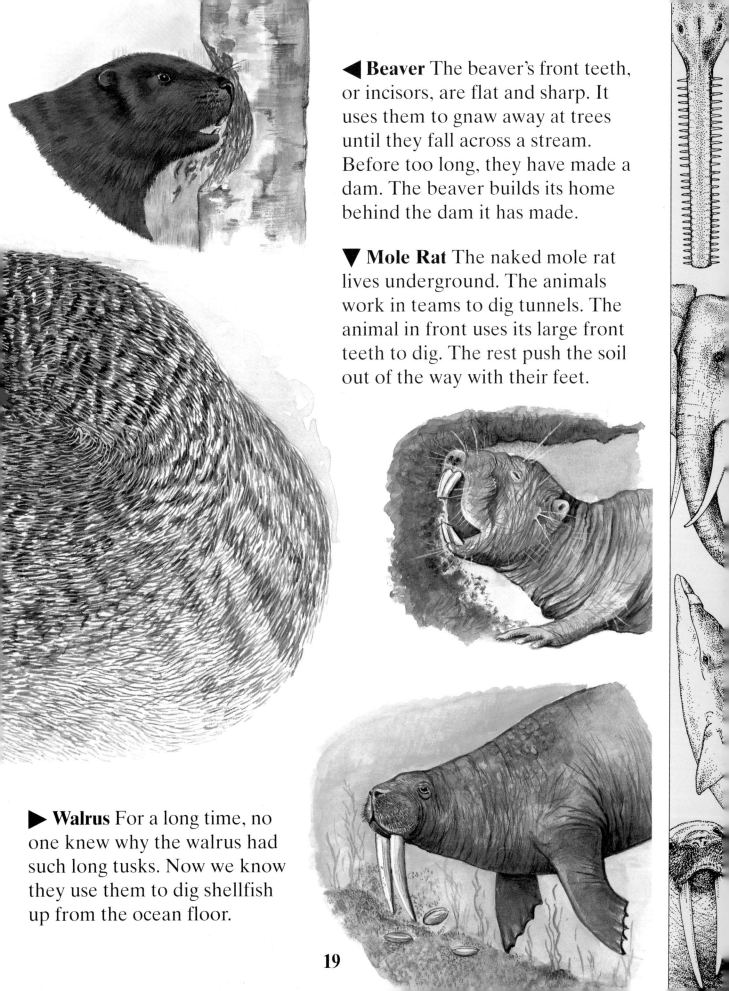

**Beaver** The beaver's front teeth, or incisors, are flat and sharp. It uses them to gnaw away at trees until they fall across a stream. Before too long, they have made a dam. The beaver builds its home behind the dam it has made.

**Mole Rat** The naked mole rat lives underground. The animals work in teams to dig tunnels. The animal in front uses its large front teeth to dig. The rest push the soil out of the way with their feet.

**Walrus** For a long time, no one knew why the walrus had such long tusks. Now we know they use them to dig shellfish up from the ocean floor.

# Scrape and Strain

Some plants and animals are too small to see. They live on stones in ponds and in the water. Some animals scrape off food from rocks, plants, or other animals. They have special teeth to do this. Other animals strain food from seawater.

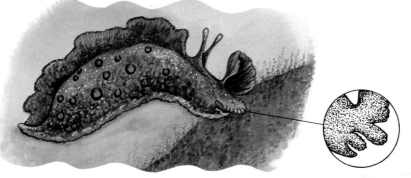

◀ **Sea Hare** The sea hare feeds on seaweed. Like the snail, it scrapes off bits of the plant and eats them.

▶ **Blue Whale** The blue whale is the largest animal on Earth. It does not have teeth. It has rows of special baleen plates. The whale sucks in a mouthful of seawater. It then forces the water through these plates. There are tiny plantlike algae and animals in the water. These get caught in the plates. The whale licks them off and swallows them.

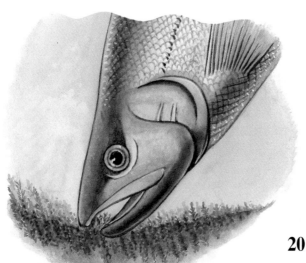

◀ **Ayu** The ayu is a river and ocean fish. It scrapes off the plantlike algae that grow on rocks at the bottom of the water. Then it strains out the water and eats the algae.

▼ **Snail** A snail has thousands of tiny teeth. They lie in rows along a kind of tongue. The snail uses its teeth to scrape off bits of plants.

▼ **Lamprey** The lamprey is a small fish. It clings to larger fish with its mouth. Inside its mouth are rows of small teeth. These scrape off bits of the fish, which the lamprey then eats.

# Poison!

Some hunters kill their prey with poison. Spiders and snakes are such hunters. They bite their prey with their sharp fangs. Then, with their fangs, they squirt poison into the animal. This kills the animal or stops it from moving. The hunter then eats its prey.

▶ **Gila Monster** Don't play with a gila monster! This lizard can give you a very painful bite. The pain from the bite is made worse by the poison the lizard makes. The poison flows along a groove in the gila monster's tooth. It uses its poison to kill the small animals it eats.

▶ **Black Widow Spider** No one wants to meet a black widow spider. Its poison is strong enough to make a person very sick. They can even die. Why is its poison so strong? No one knows. The spider is small and could not eat a person.

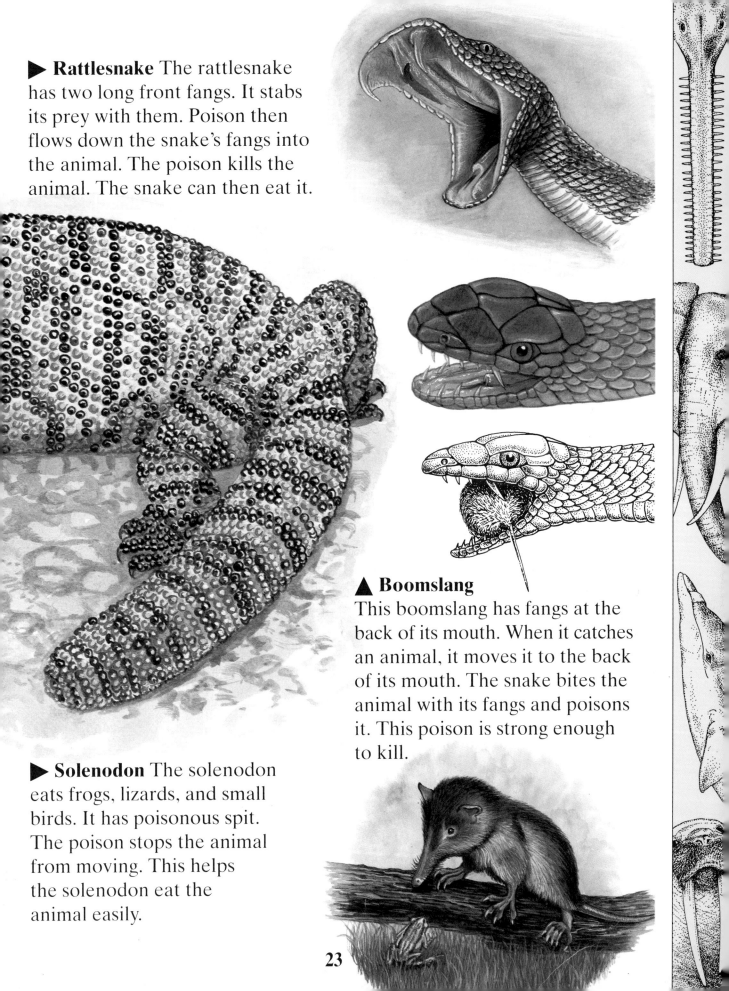

▶ **Rattlesnake** The rattlesnake has two long front fangs. It stabs its prey with them. Poison then flows down the snake's fangs into the animal. The poison kills the animal. The snake can then eat it.

▲ **Boomslang**
This boomslang has fangs at the back of its mouth. When it catches an animal, it moves it to the back of its mouth. The snake bites the animal with its fangs and poisons it. This poison is strong enough to kill.

▶ **Solenodon** The solenodon eats frogs, lizards, and small birds. It has poisonous spit. The poison stops the animal from moving. This helps the solenodon eat the animal easily.

# A Tough Job

Leaves, stems, and roots of plants are very tough. Animals that eat plants need big molars with flat tops to grind them. Some animals have hard ridges on their teeth. They move their teeth from side to side to grind up the plants. Animals that eat grass often do not have canine teeth. They would just get in the way.

▶ **Giant Panda** The giant panda eats over 30 pounds (14 kg) of bamboo every day. It has very strong jaws and teeth to grind up the stems.

◀ **Rabbit** Rabbits are always munching. This jack rabbit eats buds and shoots, as well as grass. It bites off a mouthful with its sharp front teeth. Then it grinds up the food with its flat molars.

▶ **Goat** Watch the way a goat eats. Its jaws move from side to side. It is grinding up its food. A goat will eat anything. Grass, flowers, fruits, cake, and sugar lumps. Even tough things like bark or your jeans appeal to a goat.

24

▼ **Zebra** The zebra lives in Africa. It eats tough, dry grass. It uses its large, strong molars to grind up the grass.

▼ **Rhinoceros** The huge black rhinoceros eats plants. It grasps the ends of twigs with its lips. Then it pulls the plants into its mouth. The black rhino uses its large back teeth to grind up its food.

# Open Up!

Do you like eating nuts? So do some other animals. They don't have a nutcracker, so they use their teeth. Other animals eat things such as beetles, cockroaches, and snails. They also have hard shells. An animal has to break open the shell to get at the food.

▶ **Bats** The greater horseshoe bat eats beetles it catches in midair. It breaks them open with its sharp teeth.

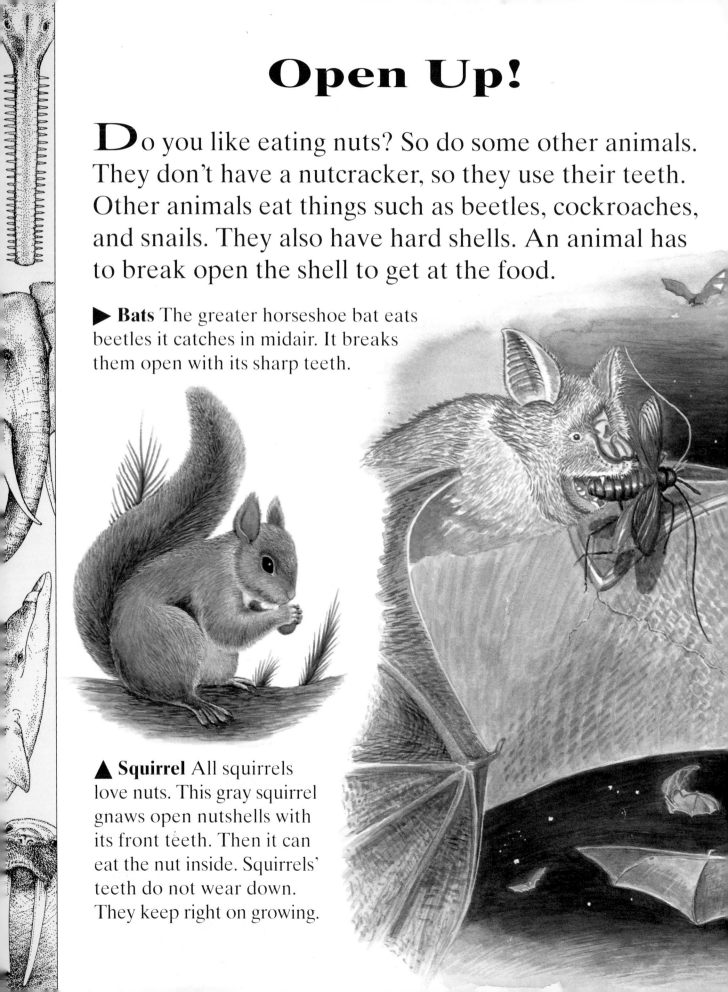

▲ **Squirrel** All squirrels love nuts. This gray squirrel gnaws open nutshells with its front teeth. Then it can eat the nut inside. Squirrels' teeth do not wear down. They keep right on growing.

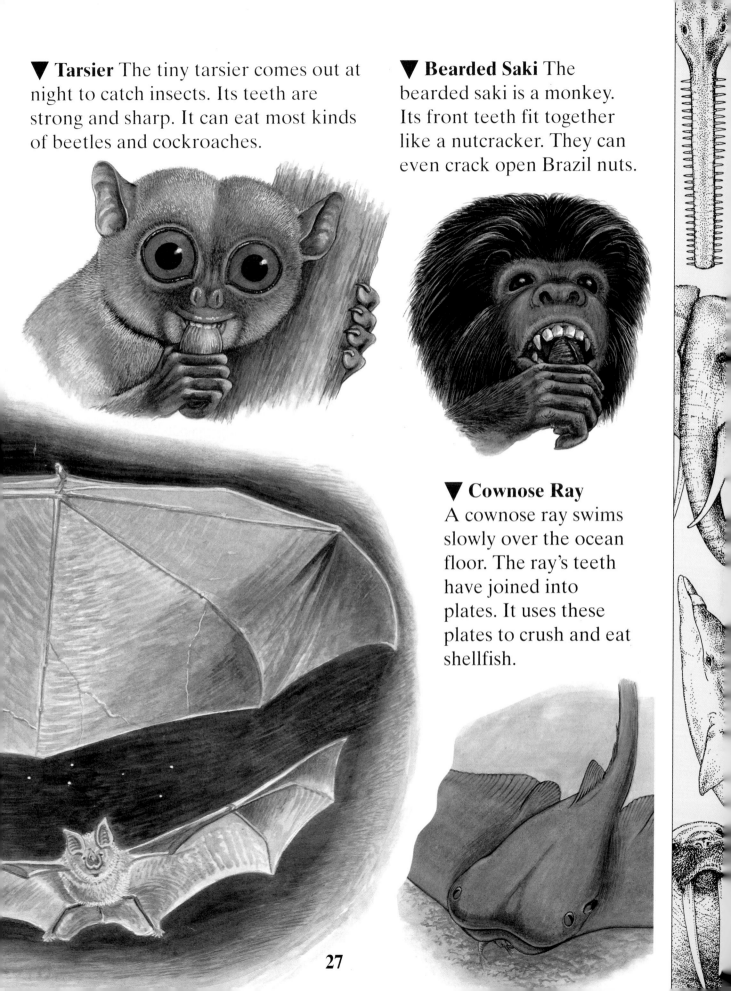

▼ **Tarsier** The tiny tarsier comes out at night to catch insects. Its teeth are strong and sharp. It can eat most kinds of beetles and cockroaches.

▼ **Bearded Saki** The bearded saki is a monkey. Its front teeth fit together like a nutcracker. They can even crack open Brazil nuts.

▼ **Cownose Ray** A cownose ray swims slowly over the ocean floor. The ray's teeth have joined into plates. It uses these plates to crush and eat shellfish.

# Hold Tight!

Fish are covered with slime. This makes them very hard to hold. They wiggle and slide away. Many fish eat other kinds of fish. These hunting fish have very sharp teeth to hold onto their prey.

▶ **Viper Fish** The deep-sea viper fish has fangs like needles. Its mouth can stretch open like a bag. It can swallow fish larger than itself!

▲ **Pike** A pike is a very fierce fish. It has sharp teeth on the roof of its mouth and in its jaws. A pike will catch fish and ducklings.

▼ **Sand Tiger**
The sand tiger shark's long teeth curve backward. It can catch very slippery things, such as small fish and squid.

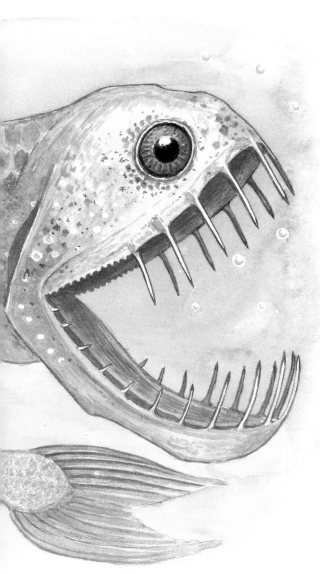

▼ **Garfish** The garfish has a long, narrow snout. It has rows of teeth in its mouth. The garfish snaps up little fish that swim near the surface of the ocean. The rows of teeth stop fish from wiggling back out.

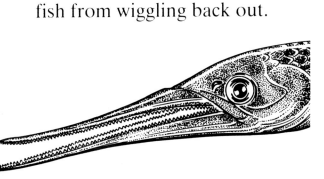

▼ **Piranha** The tiny piranha is very fierce, with sharp teeth. It often eats other fish. A group of piranhas will attack much larger animals. Each fish darts at the animal and takes a bite. They can eat an animal in minutes.

# Look at Me!

**M**ale animals often "show off" to win a female. Two males will even have pretend fights. Some just make fierce faces to scare away another male.

▼ **Wapiti** Stags such as these wapiti put their heads down and lock their antlers. They push one another to see who is the strongest.

▶ **Stag Beetle** The jaws of this beetle look a little like antlers. They are too weak to bite with. So they use them to fight. The winner is the beetle that flips the other onto its back.

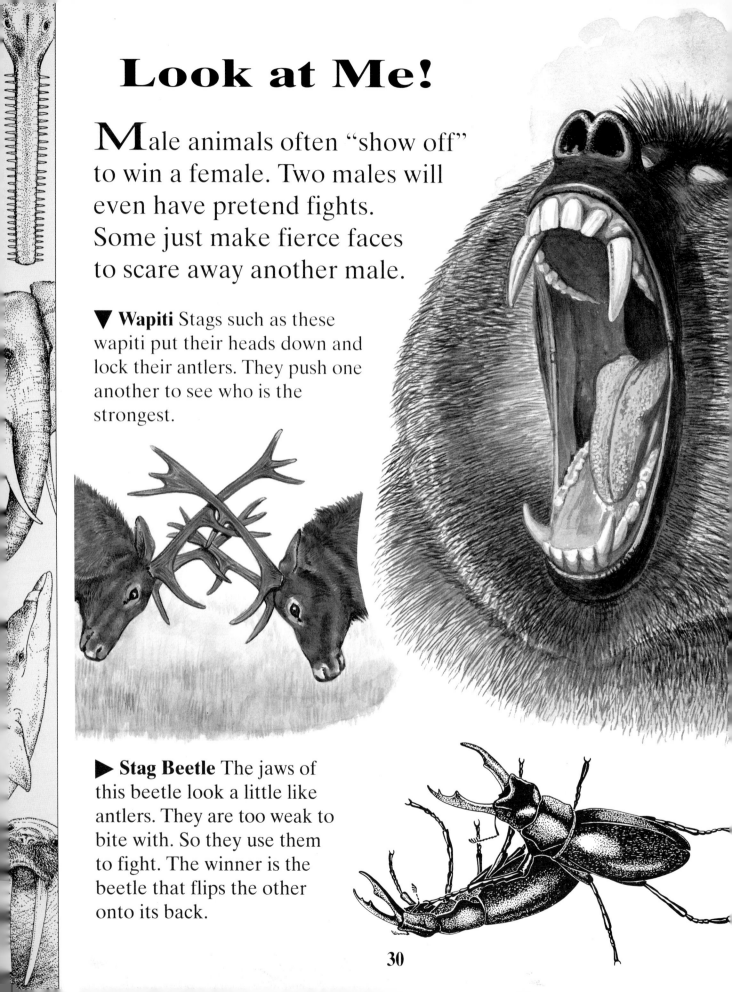

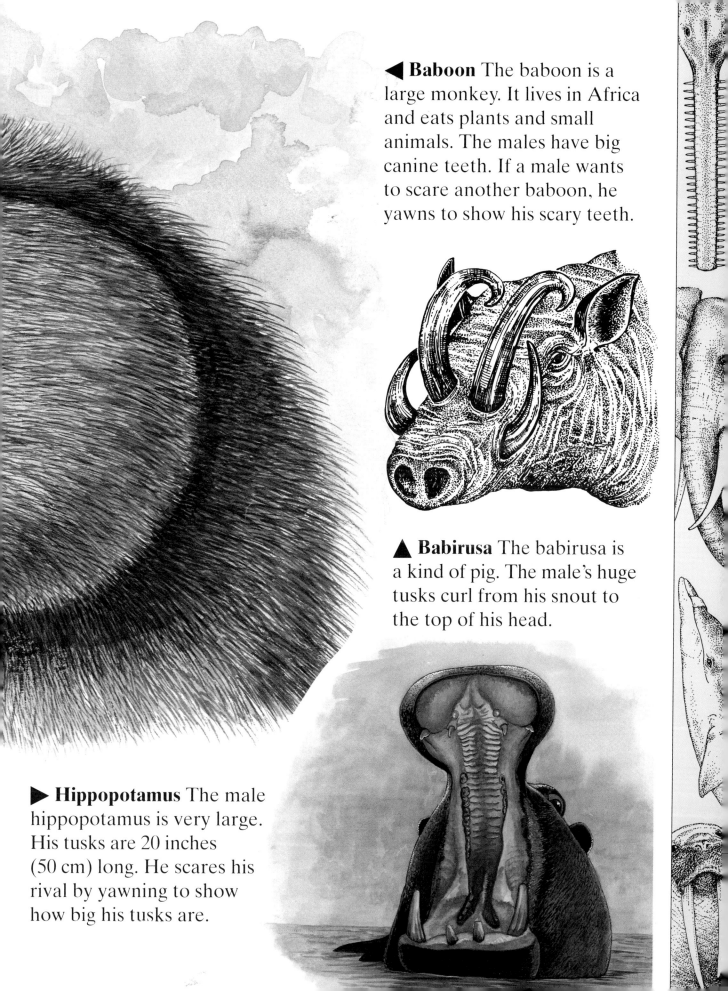

**◀ Baboon** The baboon is a large monkey. It lives in Africa and eats plants and small animals. The males have big canine teeth. If a male wants to scare another baboon, he yawns to show his scary teeth.

**▲ Babirusa** The babirusa is a kind of pig. The male's huge tusks curl from his snout to the top of his head.

**▶ Hippopotamus** The male hippopotamus is very large. His tusks are 20 inches (50 cm) long. He scares his rival by yawning to show how big his tusks are.

# New Teeth for Old

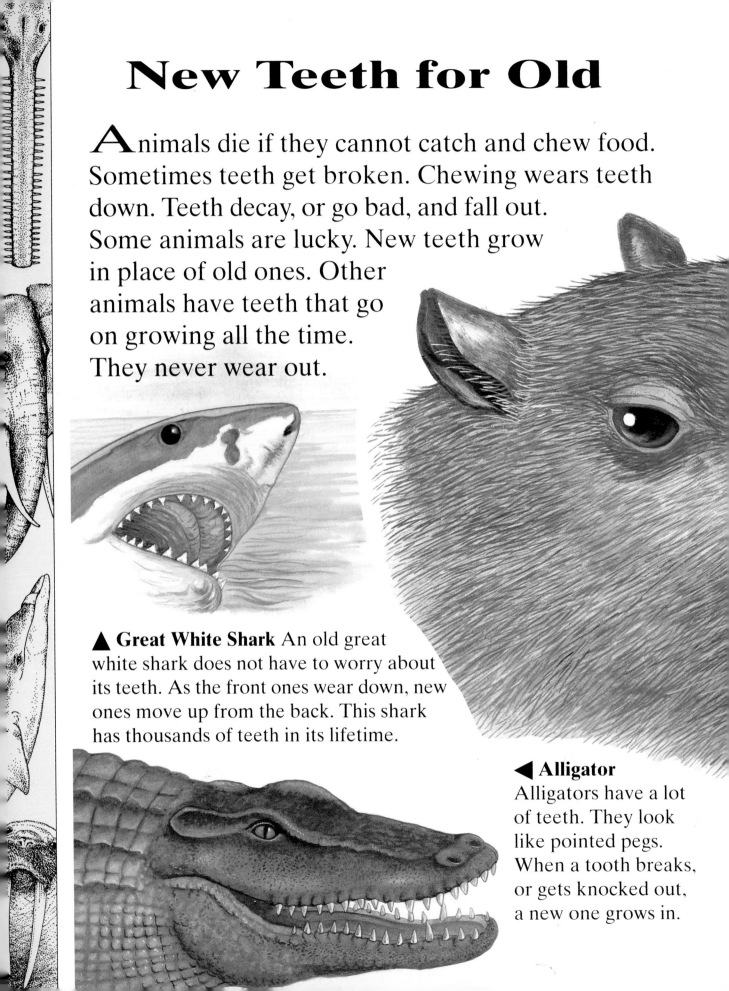

Animals die if they cannot catch and chew food. Sometimes teeth get broken. Chewing wears teeth down. Teeth decay, or go bad, and fall out. Some animals are lucky. New teeth grow in place of old ones. Other animals have teeth that go on growing all the time. They never wear out.

▲ **Great White Shark** An old great white shark does not have to worry about its teeth. As the front ones wear down, new ones move up from the back. This shark has thousands of teeth in its lifetime.

◀ **Alligator**
Alligators have a lot of teeth. They look like pointed pegs. When a tooth breaks, or gets knocked out, a new one grows in.

**▼ Capybara** Your teeth are white. The capybara has bright orange teeth. Its teeth grow throughout its life.

**▲ Dugong** The dugong is cousin to the manatee. It lives in the water as well. It does not keep making new teeth. A dugong's teeth go on growing. If it stopped chewing, they would grow too long!

**▶ Manatee** This manatee eats water plants. As old front teeth drop out, new ones move from the back to take their place.

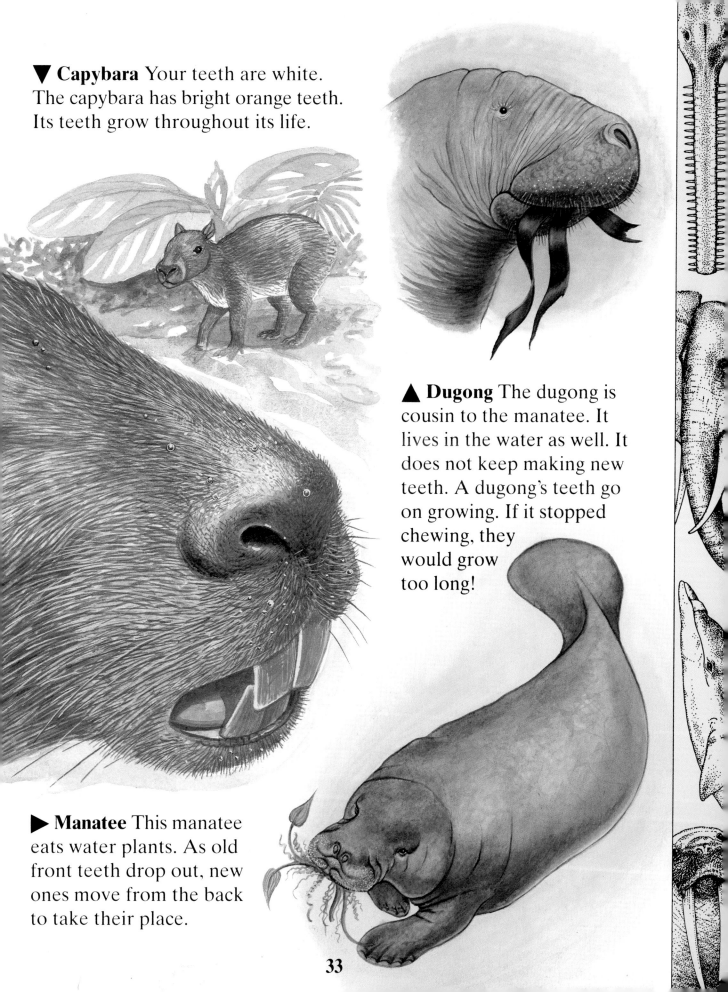

33

# Quiz

**1. How does a rattlesnake kill its prey?**

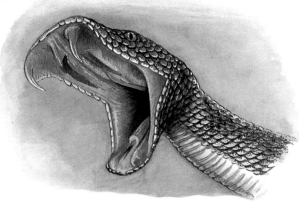

**2. Why is this hippopotamus yawning?**

**3. Which animals do these tusks belong to?**

**(a)**

**(b)**

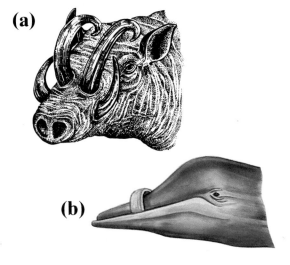

**4. Which animals do these teeth belong to?**

**(a)**

**(b)**

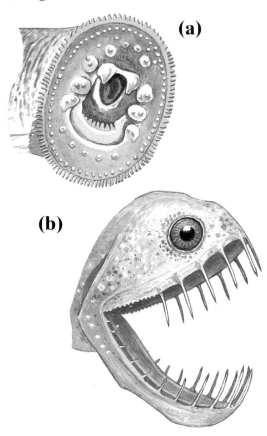

**5. What does a tiger eat?**

34

**6. How does a mole rat dig its tunnels?**

**7. Why can the zebra eat tough, dry grass?**

**8. This little pudu has the smallest antlers. Which living deer has the largest antlers?**

**9. What does a goat eat?**

**10. What does a walrus use its tusks for?**

**11. Does a female caribou have antlers?**

If you do not know the answers turn to the following pages:
**1.** p23, **2.** p31, **3a.** p31, **3b.** p9, **4a.** p21, **4b.** p29, **5.** p12, **6.** p19, **7.** p25, **8.** p11, **9.** p24, **10.** p19, **11.** p11

# Glossary

**Algae** A group of plantlike living things. Many algae live in salt and fresh water.

**Antlers** Sharp pointed bonelike structures that grow from a male deer's head. Antlers are often branched. Every year antlers fall off, and new ones grow. They usually get larger each year.

**Baleen plates** Not all whales have teeth. Instead some whales have strips of a tough material, called baleen, hanging down from the roof of their mouth. These strips of baleen have fringed edges. The baleen plates act like a strainer. The whale takes in a mouthful of seawater. Then it partly closes its mouth and forces the water out through the baleen plates. Small animals and algae in the water get caught. The whale then licks this food off the plates with its tongue and swallows it.

**Canines** Sharp pointed teeth near the front of the mouth.

**Dam** A structure built across a river that keeps the water from flowing downstream.

**Dentine** The very hard bonelike material that teeth are made from.

**Desert** A place where rain hardly ever falls. Deserts are so dry that very few animals and plants can live there.

**Enamel** The hard, shiny material that covers and protects teeth.

**Fangs** Extra-long, extra-sharp teeth, usually at the front of the mouth.

**Frog** An animal that lives part of its life in water and part on land. A frog has a small body, with smooth, wet skin. It has small front legs and large back legs. The adult frog has no tail.

**Grind** To crush tough food such as grass between flat-topped teeth. This breaks the food up into tiny pieces. Then the animal can swallow it.

**Incisors** The flat teeth at the front of the mouth.

**Jaws** The bones of the head that contain the teeth. Also, the parts of the mouth used by small animals such as insects to eat their food.

**Lizard** A lizard is an animal with a scaly skin. Most lizards have four legs. They belong to a group of animals called reptiles.

**Marsupial** An animal that carries its very tiny babies in a special pouch. Marsupial animals include kangaroos, koalas, and wombats.

**Molars** The teeth at the sides of the mouth. In some animals the molars are flat and ridged. They are used to grind up food. Some meat-eating animals have sharp scissorlike molars for slicing up their food. Others have very strong molars for breaking open and crunching up bones.

**Poison** A substance that can harm an animal.

**Predator** An animal that kills and eats other animals.

**Prey** An animal that is killed and eaten by another animal.

**Snake** A scaly animal that does not have any legs. It moves by wiggling over the ground. Snakes belong to the group of animals called reptiles.

**Territory** An area that an animal lives in. Some animals defend their territory from animals of the same kind.

**Tusks** Extra-large teeth that can be seen when an animal's mouth is shut. Elephants and walruses have tusks.

# Index

**A TEMPLAR BOOK**

Devised and produced by The Templar Company plc
Pippbrook Mill, London Road, Dorking,
Surrey RH4 1JE, Great Britain